Earth's Amazing Animals

Animal Superpowers

DEADLY WEAPONS

Joanne Mattern

RED CHAIR
PRESS

Animal Superpowers is produced and published by Red Chair Press:

Red Chair Press LLC   PO Box 333   South Egremont, MA 01258-0333

www.redchairpress.com

Publisher's Cataloging-In-Publication Data
Names: Mattern, Joanne, 1963-

Title: Deadly weapons / Joanne Mattern.

Other Titles: Core content library.

Description: South Egremont, MA : Red Chair Press, [2019] | Series: Earth's amazing animals : animal superpowers | Includes glossary, Power Word science term etymology, fact and trivia sidebars. | Includes bibliographical references and index. | Summary: "Strong jaws, razor-sharp teeth, exploding gases! Discover some of the super weapons in Earth's animal kingdom."--Provided by publisher.

Identifiers: LCCN 2018937236 | ISBN 9781634404204 (library hardcover) | ISBN 9781634404266 (ebook)

Subjects: LCSH: Animal defenses--Juvenile literature. | Animals--Juvenile literature. | CYAC: Animal defenses. | Animals.

Classification: LCC QL751.5 .M381 2019 (print) | LCC QL751.5 (ebook) | DDC 591.47--dc23

Illustrations by Tim Haggerty

Maps by Joe LeMonnier

Photo credits: iStock except Alamy, pg. 14

Printed in United States of America

102018 1P CGBS19

Table of Contents

Introduction

It's no surprise that animals have to defend themselves. Animals fight off enemies in different ways. Some animals use their teeth to give a painful bite. Others have sharp claws. Some animals are poisonous. Others have powerful bodies that can fight off **predators**.

Many animals have strong **defenses**. But some animals go even further. These animals defend themselves with weapons that are deadly, horrifying, or just plain weird. Like the superheroes in movies and comics, many animals have developed superpowers to stay safe from danger. Let's take a look at some of the super-deadly animals on our planet.

Pretty Deadly: The Poison Dart Frog

Poison dart frogs look pretty. They come in bright colors, including blue, orange, green, and yellow. But those pretty colors are really a warning. It's a great idea to stay away from this **amphibian**. Why? It is one of the most poisonous animals on Earth.

Poison dart frogs secrete a **toxin** through their skin. Any animal that eats one of these frogs is in for a nasty surprise! These animals don't just taste bad. Their poison can kill a predator. One species, called the golden poison dart frog, has enough toxins to kill 20,000 mice. It could also kill 10 adult humans!

Golden poison dart frog

Power Word: From the Greek words *amphi* and *bios* meaning both kinds of life, amphibians live in both water and on land.

Scientists are looking at ways to use the frog's poison as medicine for people.

Poison dart frogs come in many colors.

Poison dart frogs live in Central and South America. The climate there is warm and wet all year long. The warm weather means there is plenty of food for these frogs to eat. Poison dart frogs eat insects. They slurp up their **prey** with their long, sticky tongues. Their diet includes fruit flies, ants, termites, and baby crickets. Most importantly, these frogs eat tiny beetles. These beetles are filled with poison from the plants they eat. The poison from the beetles stays in the frog's body. The frog then uses that poison to defend itself.

Super Jaws:
The Komodo Dragon

When it comes to big, bad, and deadly, few animals are as dangerous as the Komodo dragon. This **reptile** lives on four islands in Indonesia. The Komodo is the largest lizard in the world. A male can measure up to 8.5 feet (2.6 m) long and weigh more than 200 pounds (90 kg).

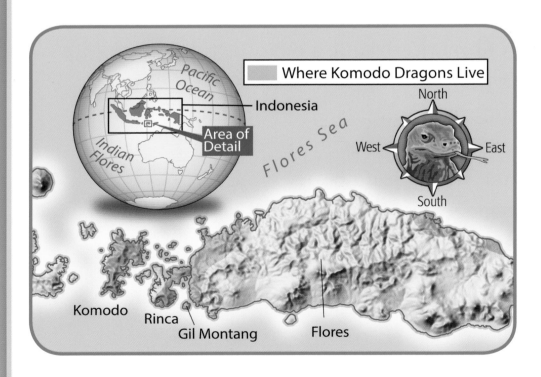

Komodo dragon

A Komodo dragon's deadliest weapon is its mouth. This **carnivore** eats many different animals. The dragon is strong enough to kill even large animals, like water buffalo and wild pigs. The dragon even eats its prey's horns and hooves.

A Komodo dragon can run very fast. These reptiles chase down their prey. Then they bite it with their strong jaws. A Komodo dragon's bite is **venomous**. Its prey might escape, but it will soon die. The dragon tracks its dying prey with its powerful sense of smell. Once its prey is dead, the Komodo dragon feasts on it. A Komodo dragon can eat up to 80 percent of its weight in one meal.

Now You Know!

Komodo dragons often eat their own young. Baby Komodo dragons often climb trees to escape from adult dragons that want to eat them.

Acid Attack:
The Bombardier Beetle

Most insects look small and harmless. But you would not want to fool around with a bombardier beetle! This insect has a secret weapon that creates a nasty surprise attack!

There are about 500 species of bombardier beetle. They live all over the world, on every continent except Antarctica. These insects are less than one inch (2.5 cm) long.

Bombardier beetles eat other insects. They have powerful jaws to catch and eat other beetles and insect larvae.

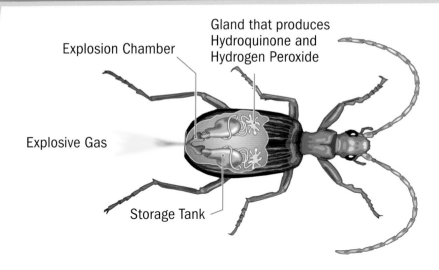

Explosion Chamber

Gland that produces Hydroquinone and Hydrogen Peroxide

Explosive Gas

Storage Tank

Like other beetles, bombardiers have a hard shell that protects them from predators. But if their shell doesn't protect them, they have an even better weapon.

When a bombardier beetle is attacked, it sets off a small chemical explosion inside its body. This explosion shoots boiling-hot acid from the beetle's **abdomen**. It also makes a loud noise. The explosion is so strong, it can kill other insects. It can also scare away large predators and burn their skin and eyes.

The bombardier is not your average beetle!

Shocking!
The Electric Eel

We don't usually think of animals having electric power. But the electric eel is a fish that can really shock you!

An electric eel has about 6000 special cells in its body. These cells are called **electrocytes**. An eel's electrocytes can produce about 600 volts of electricity. That's about five times stronger than the electricity produced in an electrical outlet in a house. An electric eel's shock is strong enough to kill a horse!

Now You Know!

A large eel could produce enough electricity to power 20 light bulbs.

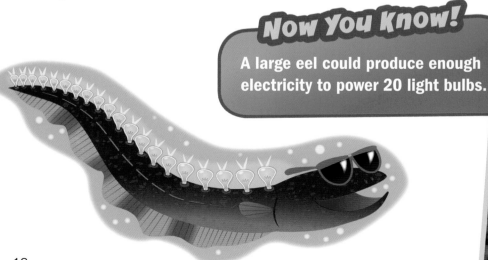

The electric eel is closely related to the catfish.

Electric eels live in shallow, muddy water in the Amazon River in South America. Eels are carnivores, or meat-eaters. They eat other fish, plus amphibians, and even birds and small mammals that come near the water.

Now You Know!

Unlike most fish, electric eels breathe air. They come to the surface about every ten minutes to breathe.

Caribbean Sea

ATLANTIC OCEAN

SURINAME

VENEZUELA

FRENCH GUIANA

GUYANA

COLOMBIA

ECUADOR

PERU

Amazon River

Amazon Basin

BRAZIL

Andes Mountains

BOLIVIA

PACIFIC OCEAN

South America

Atlantic Ocean

Pacific Ocean

North

West

East

South

Electric eels can grow to 6 to 8 feet (2 to 2.5 m) long.

Electric eels use their power to shock their prey. They also shock predators to stay safe. These eels have one more use for their electrical power. Because they have poor eyesight and live in muddy waters, electric eels can give off an electric glow that helps them see.

The Better to Eat You With:
The Piranha

Most fish don't seem scary. This is especially true of smaller fish. How dangerous can a fish be if it is only six to ten inches (15 to 25 cm) long? In the case of a piranha, pretty dangerous!

The name "piranha" means "tooth fish" in a native language in Brazil. It's easy to see why. The piranha's mouth is filled with triangle-shaped, very sharp teeth. A piranha's teeth are so sharp, they can rip flesh right off of an animal's body.

Piranhas live in rivers and marshlands in South America. They usually swim in groups of about 20 fish. Swimming in groups helps this fish stay safe from predators. A group of fish can also attack large prey.

Some kinds of piranhas eat meat. But others eat seeds and plants. Also, piranhas do not usually attack people. Still, a fish with that many sharp teeth has some very deadly weapons in its mouth!

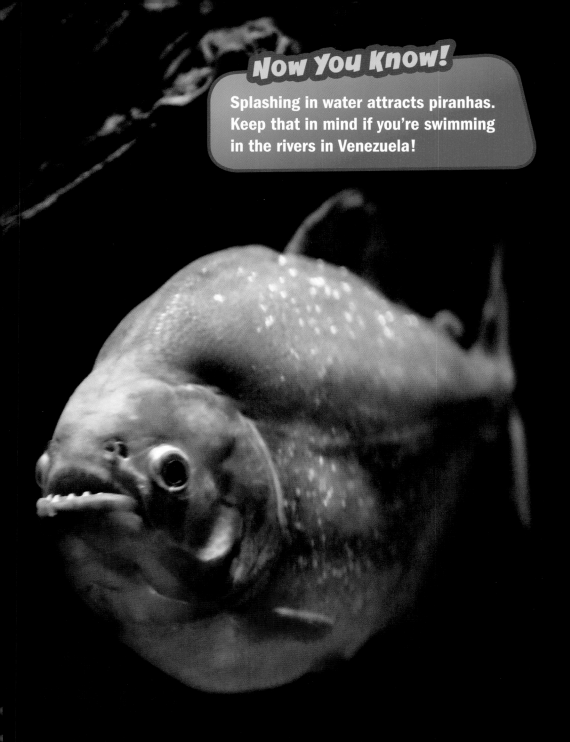

Splashing in water attracts piranhas. Keep that in mind if you're swimming in the rivers in Venezuela!

The piranha is a small but powerful fish!

Slash and Bite!
The Wolverine

You wouldn't want to fight a wolverine! These mammals have super-long claws that could rip you to shreds!

A wolverine is the largest member of the rodent family. These big, furry animals weigh between 20 and 50 pounds (9 to 20 kg). They are about three feet long. Wolverines live in cold places in North America, Russia, and northern Europe.

Now You Know!

The University of Michigan mascot is named after this powerful animal.

Wolverines weigh about 30 pounds (14 kg).

Now You Know!

A wolverine has great senses of smell and hearing, but it has terrible eyesight.

A wolverine eats many different things. Its long claws come in handy when it is hunting other animals. A wolverine's claws help it attack and kill even large animals like mountain goats and moose.

A wolverine has a special jaw. This animal's back teeth are turned sideways. This helps it tear apart its prey. A wolverine's powerful jaws and teeth can crush an animal right down to its bones.

Deadly Defenses

The animals in this book all have deadly ways to defend themselves. Some use sharp claws and teeth. Others use poison or electric shocks. These special attacks have an important job. Teeth, claws, and poison help an animal protect itself from predators. These weapons can also help animals find and kill their prey. Without these deadly weapons, some animals would have trouble finding food to eat. They would also have trouble staying safe.

It's fun to read about superheroes and their amazing powers. But don't forget, there are plenty of animals with superpowers too!

Glossary

abdomen the lower part of an insect's body

amphibians animals that spend the first part of their lives in the water and the second part on land

carnivores animals that eat other animals

defenses ways an animal protects itself

electrocytes cells in a fish's body that give off an electric charge

predators animals that hunt other animals for food

prey animals that are hunted by other animals for food

reptile an animal that is cold-blooded, has scaly skin, and lays eggs

toxin poison

venomous poisonous

Learn More in the Library

Hirsch, Rebecca E. *Exploding Ants and Other Amazing Defenses.* Lerner, 2017.

Riehecky, Janet. *Teeth, Claws, and Jaws: Animal Weapons and Defenses.* Capstone Press, 2012.

Smithsonian Zoo
https://nationalzoo.si.edu/animals/electric-eel

Index

About the Author

Joanne Mattern is the author of nearly 350 books for children and teens. She began writing when she was a little girl and just never stopped! Joanne loves nonfiction because she enjoys bringing science topics to life and showing young readers that nonfiction is full of compelling stories! Joanne lives in the Hudson Valley of New York State with her husband, four children, and several pets!